弟ㄉㄧˋ子ㄗˇ規ㄍㄨㄟ
dì　　zǐ　　guī

南海岸中華文化中心暨爾灣中文學校出版

美商EHGBooks微出版公司
www.EHGBooks.com

EHG Books 公司出版
Amazon.com 總經銷
2018 年版權美國登記
未經授權不許翻印全文或部分
及翻譯為其他語言或文字
2018 年 EHGBooks 第一版

Copyright © 2018 by

South Coast Chinese Culture Center

Irvine Chinese School

Manufactured in the United States

Permission required for reproduction,

or translation in whole or part.

Contact: info@EHGBooks.com

ISBN-13：978-1-62503-459-5

序
Introduction

　　《弟子規》，原名《訓蒙文》，出現於清朝時期。原著多被認為是清朝康熙年間的秀才李毓秀，後經清朝乾隆辛卯科副榜賈存仁修訂改編、更名為《弟子規》。

　　《弟子規》內容取自《論語・學而篇》中的第六條：「弟子入則孝，出則弟，謹而信，汎愛眾，而親仁，行有餘力，則以學文。」以三字一句，兩句一韻的文體方式編纂而成。全文共360句、1080個字，分為七個部分：《總敘》、《入則孝》、《出則弟》、《謹》、《信》、《汎愛眾》、《親仁》以及《餘力學文》，核心思想是孝、悌、仁、愛。

　　學習《弟子規》能幫助學生認識中華傳統的倫理道德知識、訓誡弟子在日常生活中應當遵循的規範。

　　Di Zi Gui was written by Li Yuxiu in the Qing Dynasty (1661-1722). The book is based on the ancient teaching of the Chinese philosopher Confucius and emphasizes the basic requisites for being a good person and guideline for living in harmony with others.

關於爾灣中文學校

　　南海岸中華文化協會是一個成立於一九七七年的非營利組織。我們的宗旨是為促進各族裔對中華文化的認識，保存及宣揚中華文化的傳統。在南海岸中華文化協會歷屆理事會和所有會員及爾灣中文學校全體教職員、以及師生們的三十多年共同奮鬥下，我們成功的建立了自己真正的家－－位於爾灣市宏偉壯觀的南海岸中華文化中心。

　　南海岸中華文化協會的會員家庭主要分佈在橙郡各縣市內。協會重視會員間彼此的交誼及輔助爾灣中文學校，同時推廣華人社區的主要社團活動。協會不遺餘力地舉辦多項有助於身心健康的社區活動，以便家長及會員們在一星期繁忙緊張的工作後，能與一群志同道合的朋友們，在歡笑中舒展身心、增進情誼。南海岸文化中心於二〇〇五年開幕後，至今已開設一百多項具多元文化的綜合課程及活動，諸如：中文、日文、韓文、國學經典讀書會、中文電腦班、合唱團、中西音樂班、太極功夫、國畫、書法、中國結、棋藝、瑜珈術、有氧舞蹈、民族舞蹈、土風舞、踢踏舞、卡拉OK歌唱、聯誼舞會、羽毛球、乒乓球、籃球及多樣性的大型晚會等。

　　南海岸中華文化協會更肩負起對外溝通聯繫的重任，積極參與贊助南加州社會各層面，包括主流及華裔社區各項比賽及活動，並舉辦學術文化交流的講座及節目。本著熱心誠懇與努力不懈的態度，及在校長、全體師生、家長及理事會共同的奮鬥下，使得爾灣中文學校及南海岸中華文化協會屢屢獲獎，並得到一致的讚譽，成為南加州極具代表性的組織。

　　南海岸中華文化協會一向積極及熱心參與與主流社區的交流活動，近年來南加州主流與各族裔也頻頻主動接觸我們，顯示出我們努力的成果，以及華人的影響力與政治力量是絕對不容輕忽的。我們會以真誠及熱情來加強社區間的多元文化交流，使得更多人瞭解及分享中華文化五千年悠久的歷史。

　　承先啟後，繼往開來，感謝前輩們的高瞻遠矚及深思熟慮，在歷屆理事會、爾灣中文學校及家長會的苦心經營和社會熱心人士和廠商的慷慨贊助下我們才會有今天的成果。在此謹向歷年來在財力、物力、人力與提供各種資源的熱心支持者，致上最崇高的敬意。我們也誠摯的歡迎志同道合的朋友，加入並且壯大協會的行列，並且貢獻一己之力，為在美華人及我們的下一代，創造更美好的明天。

目 錄

總　敘 …………………………… 2

入則孝 …………………………… 3

出則弟 …………………………… 17

謹 …………………………… 28

信 …………………………… 45

汎愛眾 …………………………… 60

親　仁 …………………………… 75

餘力學文 …………………………… 79

總敘【1】

弟子規　聖人訓
首孝弟　次謹信

繁

jiǎn 简

dì zǐ guī　shèng rén xūn
弟 子 规　圣 人 训
shǒu xiào tì　cì jǐn xìn
守 孝 弟　次 谨 信

　Di Zi Gui teaches us how to be dutiful to our parents and to love our siblings; and be cautious with all matters in life and how to be a trustworthy person; and believe in the teachings of the ancient Chinese scholars.

1

總敘【2】

繁

汎(ㄈㄢˋ)愛(ㄞˋ)眾(ㄓㄨㄥˋ) 而(ㄦˊ)親(ㄑㄧㄣ)仁(ㄖㄣˊ)
有(ㄧㄡˇ)餘(ㄩˊ)力(ㄌㄧˋ) 則(ㄗㄜˊ)學(ㄒㄩㄝˊ)文(ㄨㄣˊ)

简

fàn ài zhòng　ér qīn rén
泛 爱 众　而 亲 仁
yǒu yú lì　zé xué wén
有 余 力　则 学 文

It teaches us to love all equally, to be close to people of virtue and compassion. After we have accomplished all the above, we then can study literature and art to improve the quality of our cultural and spiritual lives.

入則孝【1】

父母呼　應勿緩
父母命　行勿懶

fù mǔ hū　yìng wù huǎn
父 母 呼　应 勿 缓
fù mǔ mìng　xíng wù lǎn
父 母 命　行 勿 懒

When your parents call you, you will respond right away. When they ask you to do something, you will do it quickly without delay.

入則孝【2】

繁

父母教 須敬聽
父母責 須順承

简

fù mǔ jiào xū jìng tīng
父 母 教 须 敬 听
fù mǔ zé xū shùn chéng
父 母 责 须 顺 承

When your parents instruct you, you will listen respectfully. When your parents reproach you, you will obey and accept their discipline and try hard to change and improve yourself.

冬則溫　夏則凊
晨則省　昏則定

dōng zé wēn　xià zé jìng
冬 則 溫　夏 則 凊
chén zé xǐng　hūn zé dìng
晨 則 省　昏 則 定

　You will make sure your parents are warm in the winter and cool in the summer. You will always greet your parents in the morning to show that you care and you will always make sure your parents rest well at night.

入則孝【4】

繁: 出必告 反必面
居有常 業無變

出必告 反必面
chū bì gào fǎn bì miàn
居有常 业无变
jū yǒu cháng yè wú biàn

You will inform your parents when you go somewhere. You must go to see your parents after you return so they do not worry about you. You will maintain a permanent place to stay and lead a routine life, including a persisting job and will not easily change your aspirations.

入則孝 【5】

事雖小 勿擅為
苟擅為 子道虧

shì suī xiǎo　wù shàn wéi
事 虽 小　勿 擅 为
gǒu shàn wéi　zǐ dào kuī
苟 擅 为　子 道 亏

If a trivial matter is wrongful and unfair to another person, you must not do it thinking it will bear no consequence. If you do, you are not being a dutiful child because your parents would not want to see you doing illegal things.

繁

物雖小 勿私藏
苟私藏 親心傷

简

wù suī xiǎo　wù sī cáng
物 虽 小　勿 私 藏
gǒu sī cáng　qīn xīn shāng
苟 私 藏　亲 心 伤

Even though an object might be small, you will not hide it just like keeping a secret from your parents from minor matters. If you do, you will hurt your parents' feelings. They will be saddened by your actions when you behave secretively.

親所好　力為具
親所惡　謹為去

qīn suǒ hào　lì wèi jù
亲　所　好　力　为　具
qīn suǒ wù　jǐn wèi qù
亲　所　恶　谨　为　去

　Anything that is legitimate and reasonable that your parents like, you will do your best to attain it for them. You should lead your parents to proper views and you will cautiously keep anything away from them if it displeases your parents.

繁

身有傷　貽親憂
德有傷　貽親羞

简

shēn yǒu shāng yí qīn yōu
身　有　伤　贻　亲　忧
dé yǒu shāng yí qīn xiū
德　有　伤　贻　亲　羞

When your body is injured, your parents will be worried. If your virtues are damaged, your parents will feel ashamed.

親愛我 孝何難
親憎我 孝方賢

qīn ài wǒ　xiào hé nán
亲 爱 我　孝 何 难
qīn zēng wǒ　xiào fāng xián
亲 憎 我　孝 方 贤

It is not difficult to be dutiful when having loving parents, but if you can still be dutiful to parents who hate you, only then will you meet the standards of the Chinese scholars for being a dutiful child.

親友過　諫使更
怡吾色　柔吾聲

qīn yǒu guò　jiàn shǐ gēng
亲 友 过　谏 使 更
yí wú sè　róu wú shēng
怡 吾 色　柔 吾 声

If your parents make a mistake you will urge them to change with a kind face and a gentle voice.

諫不入　悅復諫
號泣隨　撻無怨

jiàn bú rù　yuè fù jiàn
谏不入　悦复谏
háo qì suí　tà wú yuàn
号泣随　挞无怨

If they do not accept your advice, you will wait until another better time to dissuade them using all possible ways to make them understand. You will not hold a grudge against them even if they punish me.

入則孝【12】

繁

親有疾 藥先嘗
晝夜侍 不離床

简

qīn yǒu jí　yào xiān cháng
亲　有　疾　药　先　尝
zhòu yè shì　bù lí chuáng
昼　夜　侍　不　离　床

When your parents are ill, you will taste the Chinese herbal medicine first to make sure it is well mixed, and the temperature is just right before giving it to them. You will stay by their bedside and take care of them night and day.

喪三年　常悲咽
居處變　酒肉絕

sāng sān nián　cháng bēi yè
丧 三 年　常 悲 咽
jū chù biàn　jiǔ ròu jué
居 处 变　酒 肉 绝

The first three years after your parents have passed, you will mourn and feel sad for not being able to repay them in raising me. During this period you will arrange your home to reflect your grief and sorrow and will avoid festivities and indulgence in food and alcohols.

入則孝【14】

繁

喪盡禮　祭盡誠
事死者　如事生

简

sāng jìn lǐ　jì jìn chéng
丧　尽　礼　祭　尽　诚
shì sǐ zhě　rú shì shēng
事　死　者　如　事　生

You will observe proper etiquette in arranging your parents' funerals. For all the subsequent commemorations and anniversaries held, you should show love and respect as if they were still alive.

兄道友 弟道恭

兄弟睦 孝在中

xiōng dào yǒu dì dào gōng
兄 道 友 弟 道 恭

xiōng dì mù xiào zài zhōng
兄 弟 睦 孝 在 中

Older sibling should befriend the younger ones. Younger sibling should respect and love the older ones. If you can maintain harmonious relationships with your siblings then you am being dutiful to your parents.

出則弟【2】

繁 財物輕　怨何生
　　　言語忍　忿自泯

cái wù qīng　yuǎn hé shēng
财 物 轻　 怨 何 生
yán yǔ rěn　fèn zì mǐn
言 语 忍　 忿 自 泯

When you value your familial ties more than property and money, no resentment will come between you and your siblings. When you are careful with words and hold back hurtful comments, your feelings of anger naturally die out.

或飲食 或坐走
長者先 幼者後

huò yǐn shí huò zuò zǒu
或 饮 食 或 坐 走
zhǎng zhě xiān yòu zhě hòu
长 者 先 幼 者 后

Whether you are drinking, eating, walking, or sitting down, you will let the elders go first; the younger ones should follow.

繁

長呼人　即代叫
人不在　己即到

简

zhǎng hū rén　jí dài jiào
长　呼　人　即　代　叫
rén bú zài　jǐ jí dào
人　不　在　己　即　到

When an elder is asking for someone, you will get that person for him right away. If you cannot find that person, you will immediately report back and put yourself at the elder's service instead.

稱尊長　勿呼名
對尊長　勿見能

chēng zūn zhǎng wù hū míng
称 尊 长 勿 呼 名
duì zūn zhǎng wù xiàn néng
对 尊 长 勿 见 能

When you address an elder, you should not call him by his given name. In front of an elder, you will never show off.

出则弟【6】

繁

路遇長　疾趨揖
長無言　退恭立

简

lù　yù　zhǎng　jí　qū　yī
路　遇　长　疾　趋　揖
zhǎng　wú　yán　tuì　gōng　lì
长　无　言　退　恭　立

When you meet an elder you know on the street, you will promptly clasp your hands and greet him with a bow. If he does not speak to you, you will respectfully step back and stand aside.

騎(ㄑㄧˊ)下(ㄒㄧㄚˋ)馬(ㄇㄚˇ) 乘(ㄔㄥˊ)下(ㄒㄧㄚˋ)車(ㄐㄩ)
過(ㄍㄨㄛˋ)猶(ㄧㄡˊ)待(ㄉㄞˋ) 百(ㄅㄞˇ)步(ㄅㄨˋ)餘(ㄩˊ)

繁

qí	xià	mǎ	chéng	xià	jū
骑	下	马	乘	下	车
guò	yóu	dài	bǎi	bù	yú
过	犹	待	百	步	余

You will dismount your horse or get out of the carriage when you spot an elder you know walking, and offer him a ride. If you meet an elder passing by, you will stand and wait respectfully aside until he disappears from your sight.

繁

長者立　幼勿坐
長者坐　命乃坐

zhǎng	zhě	lì	yòu	wù	zuò
长	者	立	幼	勿	坐

zhǎng	zhě	zuò	mìng	nǎi	zuò
长	者	坐	命	乃	坐

简

When an elder is standing, you will not sit. After an elder sits down, you sit only when you am told to do so.

出則弟【9】

尊長前　聲要低
低不聞　卻非宜

尊 長 前 声 要 低
zūn zhǎng qián shēng yào dī

低 不 闻 却 非 宜
dī bù wén què fēi yí

You will speak softly in front of an elder. But it is not appropriate if your voice is hard to hear.

出則弟【10】

繁

進必趨　退必遲
問起對　視勿移

简

jìn bì qū tuì bì chí
进 必 趋 退 必 迟

wèn qǐ duì shì wù yí
问 起 对 视 勿 移

You will walk briskly towards an elder when meeting him, and will not exit in haste when leaving. When answering a question, you will look at the elder who is asking you the question.

出則弟【11】

事ˋ諸ㄓㄨ父ㄈㄨˋ 如ㄖㄨˊ事ˋ父ㄈㄨˋ

事ˋ諸ㄓㄨ兄ㄒㄩㄥ 如ㄖㄨˊ事ˋ兄ㄒㄩㄥ

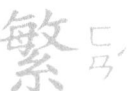

shì zhū fù rú shì fù
事 诸 父 如 事 父

shì zhū xiōng rú shì xiōng
事 诸 兄 如 事 兄

You will serve your uncles and aunts as if you are serving your parents. You will treat your cousins as if they are your own siblings.

謹【1】

繁

朝起早　夜眠遲
老易至　惜此時

zhāo qǐ zǎo　yè mián chí
朝　起　早　夜　眠　迟

lǎo yì zhì　xī cǐ shí
老　易　至　惜　此　时

You will get up before your parents each morning and you will go to bed after your parents have gone to sleep each night. When you realize that time is passing by and cannot be turned back and that you are getting older, you will especially treasure the present moment.

謹【2】

晨必盥 兼漱口
便溺回 輒淨手 繁

chén bì guàn jiān shù kǒu
晨 必 盥 兼 漱 口
biàn niào huí zhé jìng shǒu
便 溺 回 辄 净 手

After you get up in the morning, you will wash your face and brush your teeth. After going to the bathroom you will always wash your hands.

謹【3】

繁

冠必正　紐必結
襪與履　俱緊切

jiǎn 简

guān bì zhèng　niǔ bì jié
冠　必　正　　纽　必　结
wà　yǔ　lǚ　　jù　jǐn　qiē
袜　与　履　　俱　紧　切

You must wear your hat straight, and make sure the hooks of your clothes are tied and buttoned up. Your socks and shoes should also be worn neatly and correctly.

置冠服　有定位
勿亂頓　致污穢

zhì guān fú　yǒu dìng wèi
置 冠 服　有 定 位
wù luàn dùn　zhì wū huì
勿 乱 顿　致 污 秽

You will always put your hat and clothes away in their proper places. You will not carelessly throw your clothes around, for that will get them dirty.

謹【5】

繁

衣貴潔　不貴華
上循分　下稱家

简

衣貴潔　不貴華
yī guì jié　bú guì huá

上循分　下稱家
shàng xún fēn　xià chèn jiā

It is more important that your clothes are clean, rather than how extravagant they are. You will wear clothes that are suitable for your station. At home, you will wear according to your family traditions and customs.

對飲食 勿揀擇
食適可 勿過則

duì yǐn shí　wù jiǎn zé
对　饮　食　　勿　拣　择
shí shì kě　wù guò zé
食　适　可　　勿　过　则

When it comes to eating and drinking, you will not be picky. You will only eat the right amount and will not overeat.

謹【7】

繁

年方少 勿飲酒
飲酒醉 最為醜

nián fāng shǎo　wù yǐn jiǔ
年　方　少　　勿　飲　酒
yǐn jiǔ zuì　　zuì wéi chǒu
飲　酒　醉　　最　為　丑

jiǎn 简

When you are young and underage, you must not drink alcohol. When you are drunk, your behavior will turn ugly.

謹【8】

步從容 立端正
揖深圓 拜恭敬

bù cōng róng　lì duān zhèng
步 从 容　立 端 正
yī shēn yuán　bài gōng jìng
揖 深 圆　拜 恭 敬

You will walk composed, with light and even steps. You will stand with good posture. Your bows will be deep, with hands held in front and arms rounded. You will pay your respect with reverence.

謹【9】

繁

勿ㄨ 踐ㄐㄧㄢˋ 閾ㄩˋ 勿ㄨ 跛ㄅㄛˇ 倚ㄧˇ

勿ㄨ 箕ㄐㄧ 踞ㄐㄩˋ 勿ㄨ 搖ㄧㄠˊ 髀ㄅㄧˋ

简

wù jiàn yù　wù bī yi
勿 践 阈　勿 跛 倚

wù jī jù　wù yáo bì
勿 箕 踞　勿 摇 髀

You should not step on doorsill or stand leaning on one leg. You will not sit with your legs apart or sprawled out. You will not rock the lower part of your body while standing or sitting down.

緩揭簾　勿有聲
寬轉彎　勿觸棱

缓 揭 帘　勿 有 声
宽 转 弯　勿 触 棱

You will lift the curtain slowly and quietly. When you turn you will leave yourself ample space so you will not bump into a corner.

謹【11】

執虛器 如執盈
入虛室 如有人

zhí xū qì rú zhí yíng
执 虚 器 如 执 盈
rù xū shì rú yǒu rén
入 虚 室 如 有 人

You will hold empty containers carefully as if they were full. You will enter empty rooms as if they were occupied.

謹【12】

事勿忙 忙多錯
勿畏難 勿輕略

shì wù máng máng duō cuò
事 勿 忙 忙 多 错
wù wèi nán wù qīng lüè
勿 畏 难 勿 轻 略

You will avoid doing things in a hurry as it will lead to many mistakes. you should not be afraid of difficult tasks, and you will not overlook a task or become careless when it is too easy.

謹【13】

繁

鬥鬧場　絕勿近
邪僻事　絕勿問

dòu	nào	chǎng	jué	wù	jìn
斗	闹	场	绝	勿	近
xié	pì	shì	jué	wù	wèn
邪	僻	事	绝	勿	问

jiǎn 简

You will keep away from rowdy places. You will not ask about things that are abnormal or unusual.

謹【14】

將入門 問孰存
將上堂 聲必揚

jiāng rù mén wèn shú cún
将 入 门 问 孰 存
jiāng shàng táng shēng bì yáng
将 上 堂 声 必 扬

You must first ask if someone is inside before entering a main entrance. Before entering a room, you must first make yourself heard, so that those inside know someone is approaching.

謹【15】

繁 人問誰 對以名
　　 吾與我 不分明

rén wèn shuí　duì yǐ míng
人　问　谁　　对　以　名
wú　yǔ　wǒ　　bù　fēn　míng
吾　与　我　　不　分　明

简

If someone asks who you are, you must give your name. To answer 'It is me' or 'Me' is not sufficient.

謹【16】

用人物 須明求
倘不問 即為偷

Before borrowing things from others, you must ask for permission. If you do not ask, it is stealing.

谨【17】

繁:
借人物 及時還
後有急 借不難

简:
jiè rén wù　jí shí huán
借 人 物　及 时 还
hòu yǒu jí　jiè bù nán
后 有 急　借 不 难

When borrowing things from others, you will return them promptly. This will ensure that you will not have a problem borrowing from them again if you have an urgent need in the future.

凡出言　信為先
詐與妄　奚可焉

fán chū yán　xìn wéi xiān
凡 出 言　信 为 先
zhà yǔ wàng　xī kě yān
诈 与 妄　奚 可 焉

When you speak, honesty is important. Deceitful words and lies must not be tolerated.

繁

話說多 不如少
惟其是 勿佞巧

huà shuō duō bù rú shǎo
话 说 多 不 如 少

wéi qí shì wù nìng qiǎo
惟 其 是 勿 佞 巧

Rather than talking to much, it is better to speak less.
you will speak only the truth, you will not twist the facts.

信【3】

奸巧語 穢污詞
市井氣 切戒之

jiān qiǎo yǔ huì wū cí
奸 巧 语 秽 污 词
shì jǐng qì qiē jiè zhī
市 井 气 切 戒 之

Cunning words, foul language, and philistine habits must be avoided at all costs.

繁

見未真　勿輕言
知未的　勿輕傳

jiàn wèi zhēn　wù qīng yán
见　未　真　勿　轻　言

zhī wèi dì　wù qīng chuán
知　未　的　勿　轻　传

What you have not seen with your own eyes, you should not readily tell to others. What you do not know for sure, you should not easily pass on to others.

事非宜　勿輕諾
苟輕諾　進退錯

shì	fēi	yí	wù	qīng	nuò
事	非	宜	勿	轻	诺
gǒu	qīng	nuò	jìn	tuì	cuò
苟	轻	诺	进	退	错

If you are asked to do something that is inappropriate or bad, you must not agree to it. If you do, you will be doubly wrong.

繁 凡道字 重且舒
　　　 勿急疾 勿模糊

凡(fán) 道(dào) 字(zì) 重(zhòng) 且(qiě) 舒(shū)
勿(wù) 急(jí) 疾(jí) 勿(wù) 模(mó) 糊(hú)

简

You must speak clearly and to the point, and do not talk too fast nor mumble.

彼說長　此說短
不關己　莫閒管

bǐ shuō cháng　cǐ shuō duǎn
彼 说 长　此 说 短
bù guān jǐ　mò xián guǎn
不 关 己　莫 闲 管

Some like to talk about good things of others while some like to talk about the faults of others. If it is none of your business, you will not get involved.

信【8】

繁

見人善　即思齊
縱去遠　以漸躋

jiàn	rén	shàn	jí	sī	qí
见	人	善	即	思	齐

简

zòng	qù	yuǎn	yǐ	jiàn	jī
纵	去	远	以	渐	跻

When you see others doing good deeds, you should consider following their example. Even though your own achievements are still far behind those of others, you am getting closer.

見人惡　即內省
有則改　無加警

jiàn rén è　jí nèi xǐng
见　人　恶　即　内　省
yǒu zé gǎi　wú jiā jǐng
有　则　改　无　加　警

When you see others doing wrong, you must immediately reflect upon yourself. If you have made the same mistake, you should correct it. If you haven't done anything wrong, you should still take extra caution not to make the same mistake.

信【10】

繁

唯德學　唯才藝
不如人　當自礪

wéi dé xué　wéi cái yì
唯　德　学　唯　才　艺
bù rú rén　dāng zì lì
不　如　人　当　自　砺

简

When your morals, conduct, knowledge, and skills seem not as good as those of others, you will encourage yourself to be better.

信【11】

若衣服　若飲食
不如人　勿生慼

ruò yī fú　ruò yǐn shí
若　衣　服　若　饮　食
bù rú rén　wù shēng qī
不　如　人　勿　生　戚

If the clothes you wear and the food you eat are not as good as others, you should not be concerned or ashamed.

繁

聞過怒　聞譽樂
損友來　益友卻

简

闻过怒　闻誉乐
wén guò nù　wén yù lè
损友来　益友却
sǔn yǒu lái　yì yǒu què

If you don't accept criticism and you enjoy hearing compliments, bad company will come your way and good friends will shy away.

聞譽恐　聞過欣
直諒士　漸相親

闻(wén) 誉(yù) 恐(kǒng)　闻(wén) 过(guò) 欣(xīn)
直(zhí) 谅(liàng) 士(shì)　渐(jiàn) 相(xiāng) 亲(qīn)

If you hear compliments but still exam yourself and uneasy about not being good enough, and also be appreciative of criticism, then sincere, understanding, and virtuous people will gradually come close to you.

繁

無心非　名為錯

有心非　名為惡

簡

wú xīn fēi　míng wéi cuò
无　心　非　名　为　错

yǒu xīn fēi　míng wéi è
有　心　非　名　为　恶

If any mistake you make is inadvertent, it is merely a mistake. If it is done on purpose, however, it is an evil act and crime.

過能改 歸於無 繁
倘掩飾 增一辜

guò néng gǎi　guī yú wú
过 能 改　归 于 无
tǎng yǎn shì　zēng yī gū
倘 掩 饰　增 一 辜

If you correct your mistake and do not repeat it, you no longer own the mistake. If you try to cover it up, you will be doubly wrong.

汎ㄈㄢˋ愛ㄞˋ眾ㄓㄨㄥˋ【1】

繁

凡ㄈㄢˊ 是ㄕˋ 人ㄖㄣˊ 皆ㄐㄧㄝ 須ㄒㄩ 愛ㄞˋ

天ㄊㄧㄢ 同ㄊㄨㄥˊ 覆ㄈㄨˋ 地ㄉㄧˋ 同ㄊㄨㄥˊ 載ㄗㄞˋ

简

fán shì rén jiē xū ài
凡 是 人 皆 须 爱

tiān tóng Fù dì tóng zài
天 同 覆 地 同 载

Human beings should be loved equally regardless of nationality, race, or religion. You are all sheltered by the same sky and you all live on the same planet Earth.

汎[fàn]愛[ài]眾[zhòng]【2】

行[xíng]高[gāo]者[zhě]　名[míng]自[zì]高[gāo]
人[rén]所[suǒ]重[zhòng]　非[fēi]貌[mào]高[gāo]

xíng gāo zhě　míng zì gāo
行　高　者　　名　自　高
rén suǒ zhòng　fēi mào gāo
人　所　重　　非　貌　高

A person who is moral will gain reputation and be respected by others. What makes the person respectful is not based on outside appearance.

泛爱众【3】

繁

才大者 望自大
人所服 非言大

cái dà zhě wàng zì dà
才 大 者 望 自 大
rén suǒ fú fēi yán dà
人 所 服 非 言 大

简

A person's outstanding abilities will naturally endow him with a good reputation Admiration from others does not come from boasting or praising oneself.

汎ㄈㄢˋ愛ㄞˋ眾ㄓㄨㄥˋ【4】

己ㄐㄧˇ有ㄧㄡˇ能ㄋㄥˊ　勿ㄨˋ自ㄗˋ私ㄙ
人ㄖㄣˊ所ㄙㄨㄛˇ能ㄋㄥˊ　勿ㄨˋ輕ㄑㄧㄥ訾ㄗˇ

繁ㄈㄢˊ

jǐ　yǒu　néng　wù　zì　sī
己　有　能　勿　自　私
rén　suǒ　néng　wù　qīng　zǐ
人　所　能　勿　轻　訾

If you are a very capable person, you should use your capabilities to help others. Other people's competence should never be slandered easily.

泛爱众【5】

繁

勿谄富　勿骄贫

勿厌故　勿喜新

勿谄富　勿骄贫
勿厌故　勿喜新

You should not flatter the rich or despise the poor. Do not ignore old friends nor taking delight in new ones.

汎ㄈㄢˋ愛ㄞˋ眾ㄓㄨㄥˋ【6】

人ㄖㄣˊ不ㄅㄨˋ閒ㄒㄧㄢˊ　勿ㄨˋ事ㄕˋ攪ㄐㄧㄠˇ　繁ㄈㄢˊ
人ㄖㄣˊ不ㄅㄨˋ安ㄢ　勿ㄨˋ話ㄏㄨㄚˋ擾ㄖㄠˇ

rén	bù	xián	wù	shì	jiǎo
人	不	闲	勿	事	搅
rén	bù	ān	wù	huà	rǎo
人	不	安	勿	话	扰

When a person is busy, do not bother him. When a person's mind is not at ease, don't talk to him and bother him with words.

繁

人有短　切莫揭

人有私　切莫說

简

rén yǒu duǎn　qiè mò jiē
人　有　短　　切　莫　揭

rén yǒu sī　qiè mò shuō
人　有　私　　切　莫　说

If a person has a shortcoming, you should not expose it.
If a person has a secret, you should not tell others.

汎愛眾【8】

道人善 即是善
人知之 愈思勉

繁

jiǎn 简

dào rén shàn　jí shì shàn
道 人 善　即 是 善
rén zhī zhī　yù sī miǎn
人 知 之　愈 思 勉

Praising the goodness of others is a good deed in itself. When people are being praised and recognized for, they will be encouraged to try even harder.

繁

揚人惡　即是惡
疾之甚　禍且作

yáng rén è　jí shì è
扬　人　恶　即　是　恶
jí zhī shèn　huò qiě zuò
疾　之　甚　祸　且　作

简

Spreading rumors about the wrongdoings of others is a wrongdoing in itself. When the harm done has reached the extreme, misfortunes will surely follow.

善相勸　德皆建
過不規　道兩虧

善相劝　德皆建
过不规　道两亏

When you encourage another person to do good deed, both of your virtues are built up. If you do not tell another person of his faults, you are both wrong.

繁 凡取與 貴分曉
　 與宜多 取宜少

fán qǔ yǔ　guì fēn xiǎo
凡 取 与　贵 分 晓
yǔ yí duō　qǔ yí shǎo
与 宜 多　取 宜 少

Whether you take or give, you need to know the difference between the two. It is better to give more and take less.

汎愛眾【12】

將加人　先問己
己不欲　即速已

繁

jiāng　jiā　rén　xiān　wèn　jǐ
將　　加　　人　　先　　问　　己
jǐ　　bú　　yù　　jí　　sù　　yǐ
己　　不　　欲　　即　　速　　已

jiǎn
简

What you ask others to do, you must first ask yourself if you would be willing to do it. If it is not something you would be willing to do, you should not ask others to do it.

汎愛眾【13】

繁

恩欲報　怨欲忘
報怨短　報恩長

ēn yù bào　yuàn yù wàng
恩 欲 报　怨 欲 忘
bào yuàn duǎn　bào ēn cháng
报 怨 短　报 恩 长

You want to repay the kindness of others, and you should let go of your resentments. You will spend less time holding grudges and more time paying back the kindness of others.

汎愛眾【14】

待婢僕　身貴端
雖貴端　慈而寬

dài　bì　pú　shēn　guì　duān
待　婢　仆　身　贵　端
suī　guì　duān　cí　ér　kuān
虽　贵　端　慈　而　宽

When you are directing maids and servants, you will act honorably and properly. You will also treat them kindly and generously.

汎ㄈㄢˋ愛ㄞˋ眾ㄓㄨㄥˋ【15】

繁

勢ㄕˋ服ㄈㄨˊ人ㄖㄣˊ　心ㄒㄧㄣ不ㄅㄨˋ然ㄖㄢˊ

理ㄌㄧˇ服ㄈㄨˊ人ㄖㄣˊ　方ㄈㄤ無ㄨˊ言ㄧㄢˊ

shì	fú	rén	xīn	bù	rán
势	服	人	心	不	然

lǐ	fú	rén	fāng	wú	yán
理	服	人	方	无	言

简

If you use your power or influence to submit them, their hearts will not be with you. If you can convince them with sound reasoning, they will have nothing to object to.

親仁【1】

同是人　類不齊
流俗眾　仁者希

tóng shì rén　lèi bù qí
同　是　人　类　不　齐
liú sú zhòng　rén zhě xī
流　俗　众　仁　者　希

We are all human but everyone is different. Most of us are ordinary; only a very few have great virtues and high moral principles.

親仁【2】

繁

果仁者 人多畏
言不諱 色不媚

guǒ rén zhě　rén duō wèi
果 仁 者　人 多 畏
yán bú huì　sè bú mèi
言 不 讳　色 不 媚

A truly virtuous person is greatly respected by others. He will not be afraid to speak the truth and he will not fawn on others.

親(ㄑㄧㄣ) 仁(ㄖㄣˊ)【3】

能(ㄋㄥˊ)親(ㄑㄧㄣ)仁(ㄖㄣˊ)　無(ㄨˊ)限(ㄒㄧㄢˋ)好(ㄏㄠˇ)
德(ㄉㄜˊ)日(ㄖˋ)進(ㄐㄧㄣˋ)　過(ㄍㄨㄛˋ)日(ㄖˋ)少(ㄕㄠˇ)

néng qīn rén　wú xiàn hǎo
能　亲　仁　　无　限　好
dé rì jìn　guò rì shǎo
德　日　进　　过　日　少

    If you can be close to and learn from people of great virtue and compassion, you will benefit immensely. Your virtues will grow daily and your wrongdoings will lessen day by day.

親仁【4】

繁

不親仁　無限害
小人進　百事壞

簡

bù qīn rén　wú xiàn hài
不 亲 仁　无 限 害
xiǎo rén jìn　bǎi shì huài
小 人 进　百 事 坏

   If you choose not to be close to and learn from people of great virtue, you may suffer a great loss. People without virtue will get close to you and nothing you attempt will succeed.

餘⃞力⃞學⃞文⃞【1】

繁

bú	lì	xíng	dàn	xué	wén
不	力	行	但	学	文
zhǎng	fú	huá	chéng	hé	rén
长	浮	华	成	何	人

jiǎn 简

If you do not actively practice what you have learned, but continue to study on the surface, even though your knowledge is increasing, it is only superficial. What kind of person will you be?

餘力學文【2】

繁

但力行 不學文
任己見 昧理真

dàn lì xíng bù xué wén
但 力 行 不 学 文
rèn jǐ jiàn mèi lǐ zhēn
任 己 见 昧 理 真

简

If you do apply your knowledge diligently, but stop studying, you will only do things based on your own opinion, thinking it is correct. In fact, what you know is not the truth.

讀書法　有三到
心眼口　信皆要

dú shū fǎ　yǒu sān dào
读书法　有三到
xīn yǎn kǒu　xìn jiē yào
心眼口　信皆要

There are methods to study correctly. They involve concentration in three areas: your mind, your eyes, and your mouth. To believe in what you read is equally important.

繁 方讀此　勿慕彼
　　　此未終　彼勿起

简 fāng dú cǐ　wù mù bǐ
方　读　此　勿　慕　彼
cǐ wèi zhōng　bǐ wù qǐ
此　未　终　彼　勿　起

When you begin to read a book, you should not think about another. If you have not completed the book, you should not start another.

餘力學文【5】

寬為限　緊用功
工夫到　滯塞通

繁

kuān wéi xiàn　jǐn yòng gōng
宽　为　限　　紧　用　功
gōng fū dào　zhì sè tōng
工　夫　到　　滞　塞　通

Give yourself lots of time to study, but study hard and daily. If you devote enough time and effort, you will thoroughly understand the essence.

心有疑　隨札記
就人問　求確義

xīn yǒu yí　suí zhá jì
心　有　疑　随　札　记
jiù rén wèn　qiú què yì
就　人　问　求　确　义

If you have a question, make a note of it. You should also ask the person who has the knowledge for the right answer.

餘力學文【7】

房室清 牆壁淨
几案潔 筆硯正

繁

jiǎn
简

fáng shì qīng qiáng bì jìng
房 室 清 墙 壁 净
jī àn jié bǐ yàn zhèng
几 案 洁 笔 砚 正

You should keep your room neat. The walls should be uncluttered and clean. Your desk should be tidy and the brush and inkstone should be properly placed.

餘力學文【8】

繁

墨 磨 偏　心 不 端
字 不 敬　心 先 病

mò　mó　piān　xīn　bù　duān
墨　磨　偏　心　不　端
zì　bú　jìng　xīn　xiān　bìng
字　不　敬　心　先　病

jiǎn 简

If your ink block is ground unevenly, it shows you have a poor state of mind. When words are written carelessly, this shows your state of mind has not been well.

列典籍 有定處
讀看畢 還原處

liè diǎn jí   yǒu dìng chù
列 典 籍   有 定 处
dú kàn bì   huán yuán chù
读 看 毕   还 原 处

Your books should be classified, placed on the bookshelves, and in their proper places. After you finish reading a book, you will put it back where it belongs.

餘力學文【10】

繁

雖有急 卷束齊
有缺壞 就補之

suī yǒu jí juǎn shù qí
虽 有 急 卷 束 齐
yǒu quē huài jiù bǔ zhī
有 缺 坏 就 补 之

Even if you are in a hurry, you still must neatly roll up and bind the open bamboo scroll you have been reading. All missing or damaged pages ought to be immediately repaired.

非(ㄈㄟ)聖(ㄕㄥˋ)書(ㄕㄨ)　屏(ㄅㄧㄥˇ)勿(ㄨˋ)視(ㄕˋ)
蔽(ㄅㄧˋ)聰(ㄘㄨㄥ)明(ㄇㄧㄥˊ)　壞(ㄏㄨㄞˋ)心(ㄒㄧㄣ)志(ㄓˋ)

繁(ㄈㄢˊ)

fēi shēng shū　bǐng wù shì
非 圣 书　屏 勿 视
bì cōng míng　huài xīn zhì
蔽 聪 明　坏 心 志

If it is not a book on teachings of the ancient Chinese scholars, it should be discarded and not even looked at. Such books can block your intelligence and wisdom, and will undermine your aspirations and sense of direction.

繁

勿ㄨˋ自ㄗˋ暴ㄅㄠˋ　勿ㄨˋ自ㄗˋ棄ㄑㄧˋ
聖ㄕㄥˋ與ㄩˇ賢ㄒㄧㄢˊ　可ㄎㄜˇ馴ㄒㄩㄣˊ致ㄓˋ

wù zì bào　wù zì qì
勿 自 暴　勿 自 弃

shèng yǔ xián　kě xún zhì
圣 与 贤　可 驯 致

jiǎn
简

Neither be harsh on yourself, nor give up on yourself. To be a person of high ideals, moral standards and virtue is something you can all attain in time.

弟子規 Di Zi Gui

總編輯／鐘幼蘭校長

責任編輯／劉思薇

原　著／李毓秀（清）

英　譯／楊因綺

校　對／陳景星、林怡菁、陳雅娟

平面設計／劉思薇

出版者／南海岸中華文化中心暨爾灣中文學校

地　址／9 Truman, Irvine CA 92620

電　話／(949)559-6868

網　站／www.sccca.org

發行者／美商漢世紀EHGBooks微出版公司

臺灣學人出版網：http://www.TaiwanFellowship.org

印　刷／漢世紀古騰堡®數位出版POD雲端科技

出版日期／2018年9月

ISBN／978-1-62503-459-5

總經銷／Amazon.com

臺灣銷售網／三民網路書店：http://www.sanmin.com.tw

　　　　　三民書局復北店
　　　　　地址／104臺北市復興北路386號
　　　　　電話／02-2500-6600
　　　　　三民書局重南店
　　　　　地址／100臺北市重慶南路一段61號
　　　　　電話／02-2361-7511

全省金石網路書店：http://www.kingstone.com.tw

中國總代理／廈門外圖集團有限公司

地　址／廈門市湖里區悅華路8號外圖物流大廈4樓

臺灣書店購書專線／0592-5061658、6028707

定　價／新臺幣300元（美金10元 / 人民幣50元）

2018年版權美國登記，未經授權不許翻印全文或部分及翻譯為其他語言或文字。
2018　© United States, Permission required for reproduction, or translation in whole or part.

www.ingramcontent.com/pod-product-compliance
Lightning Source LLC
LaVergne TN
LVHW091604060526
838200LV00036B/986